Sometimes, it's really hard to keep track of the wins.

I've been an entrepreneur in almost as many ways as I can think of: a 5x award-winning product-based entrepreneur, vintage seller (ranking in the top 5% of sellers on Etsy), educator, blogger, podcaster, infopreneur, haphazard YouTuber. That's not to brag (or to give you a glimpse into how much coffee I consume), but rather to say that I can most likely relate to what struggles you're going through, which is why I designed this Book of Awesome for you.

My goal with this book is to help you dig out of the trenches that go along with the daily grind of creating your dream life and to gain perspective on how far you've come.

Think how far 100 steps can be down a path, how powerful 100 drops of water are in a cup, how much more 100 $1 bills can buy when combined. That's the point of this: small wins might feel small or inconsequential at the time, but together they are the tools that move your goals forward.

You're awesome, driven, and are on your way to success, so let's stop with the chit chat and get started!

Date: _____

Moment of Awesome

"Don't try to rush progress. Remember -- a step forward, no matter how small, is a step in the right direction. Keep believing."

Kara Goucher

Date: _____

Moment of Awesome

"Track your small wins to motivate big accomplishments."

Teresa Amabile

Date: _____

Moment of Awesome

"We don't have to engage in grand, heroic actions to participate in the process of change. Small acts, when multiplied by millions of people, can transform the world."

Howard Zinn

Date: _____

Moment of Awesome

"I've found that small wins, small projects, small differences often make huge differences."

Rosabeth Moss Kanter

Date: _____

Moment of Awesome

"Win small, win early, win often."

Gary Hamel

Date: _____

Moment of Awesome

"Small wins are a steady application of a small advantage."

Charles Duhigg

Date: _____

Moment of Awesome

If world problems feel too big to tackle, think small. Step by step. Small wins build confidence, lead the way to change."

Rosabeth Moss Kanter

Date: _____

Moment of Awesome

"You don't need a grand plan, you don't need to go back to the ancestors and rewrite the rules. You just need to take small steps and accumulate small wins."

Bruce Feiler

Date: _____

Moment of Awesome

"If you want to achieve excellence, you can get there today. As of this second, quit doing less-than-excellent work."

Thomas J. Watson

Date: _____

Moment of Awesome

"Champions keep playing until they get it right."

Billie Jean King

Date: _____

Moment of Awesome

"What you get by achieving your goals is not as important as what you become by achieving your goals."

Henry David Thoreau

Date: _____

Moment of Awesome

"Potential is not an endpoint but a capacity to grow and learn."

Eileen Kennedy - Moore

Date: _____

Moment of Awesome

"Your daily behavior reveals your deepest beliefs."

Robin Sharma

Date: _____

Moment of Awesome

"Success is assured when a person fears the pain of regret more than the pain of the process."

Orrin Woodward

Date: _____

Moment of Awesome

"Small daily improvements over time lead to stunning results."

Robin Sharma

Date: _____

Moment of Awesome

"All our dreams can come true if we have the courage to pursue them."

Walt Disney

Date: _____

Moment of Awesome

"Opportunities don't happen, you create them."

Chris Grosser

Date: _____

Moment of Awesome

"When your desires are strong enough, you will appear to possess superhuman powers to achieve."

Napoleon Hill

Date: _____

Moment of Awesome

"Competition is a by-product of productive work, not its goal. A creative man is motivated by the desire to achieve, not by the desire to beat others."

Ayn Rand

Date: _____

Moment of Awesome

"When you stop chasing the wrong things you give the right things a chance to catch you."

Lolly Daskal

Date: _____

Moment of Awesome

"The freedom to do your best means nothing unless you are willing to do your best."

Colin Powell

Date: _____

Moment of Awesome

"Only those who attempt the absurd can achieve the impossible."

Albert Einstein

Date: _____

Moment of Awesome

"The will to win, the desire to succeed, the urge to reach your full potential? These are the keys that will unlock the door to personal excellence."

Eddie Robinson

Date: _____

Moment of Awesome

"What the mind can conceive and believe, and the heart desire, you can achieve."

Norman Vincent Peal

Date: _____

Moment of Awesome

"The ultimate measure of a person is not her mistakes or accomplishments, but what she does with them."

Lisa M. Wiemer

Date: _____

Moment of Awesome

"There is only one thing that makes a dream impossible to achieve: the fear of failure."

Paul Coelho

Date: _____

Moment of Awesome

"When the awareness of what is achievable brushes your life, your journey has begun."

Lorii Myers

Date: _____

Moment of Awesome

"If you want to live a happy life, tie it to a goal, not to people or objects."

Albert Einstein

Date: _____

Moment of Awesome

"I feel that the greatest reward for doing is the opportunity to do more."

Jonas Salk

Date: ______________

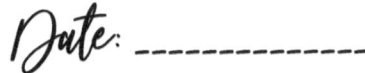

Moment of Awesome

"If the plan doesn't work, change the plan, but never the goal."

Unknown

Date: _____

Moment of Awesome

"If you are not willing to risk the usual you will have to settle for the ordinary."

Jim Rohn

Date: _____

Moment of Awesome

"What seems to us as bitter trials are often blessings in disguise."

Oscar Wilde

Date: _____

Moment of Awesome

"A successful man is one who can lay a firm foundation with the bricks others have thrown at him."

David Brinkley

Date: _____

Moment of Awesome

"The project you are most resisting carries your greatest growth."

Robin Sharma

Date: _____

Moment of Awesome

"There are two types of people who will tell you that you cannot make a difference in this world: those who are afraid to try and those who are afraid you will succeed."

Kay Goforth

Date: _____

Moment of Awesome

"Do not let what you cannot do interfere with what you can do."

John Wooden

Date: _____

Moment of Awesome

"Small wins are exactly what they sound like, and are part of how keystone habits create widespread changes."

Charles Duhigg

Date: _____

Moment of Awesome

"Yesterday is not ours to recover, but tomorrow is ours to win or lose."

Lyndon B. Johnson

Date: _____

Moment of Awesome

"I think that the power is the principle. The principle of moving forward, as though you have the confidence to move forward, eventually gives you confidence when you look back and see what you've done."

Robert Downey Jr.

Date: _____

Moment of Awesome

"If you're going through hell, keep going."

Winston Churchill

Date: _____

Moment of Awesome

"When life seems hopeless, rearrange things for a dose of dopeness."

Kid Cudi

Date: _____

Moment of Awesome

"Even if you fall on your face, you're still moving forward."

Victor Kiam

Date: _____

Moment of Awesome

"The only thing a person can ever really do is keep moving forward. Take that big leap forward without hesitation, without once looking back. Simply forget the past and forge toward the future."

Alyson Noel

Date: _____

Moment of Awesome

"If everyone is moving forward together, then success takes care of itself."

Henry Ford

Date: _____

Moment of Awesome

"When the world is at your back, and your heart is at your feet…the best way to go on is to just 'be.'"

Jennifer Varnadora

Date: _____

Moment of Awesome

"A bridge can still be built, while the bitter waters are flowing beneath."

Anthony Liccione

Date: _____

Moment of Awesome

"We must be willing to let go of the life we've planned, so as to have the life that is waiting for us."

Joseph Campbell

Date: _____

Moment of Awesome

"You've got to make a conscious choice every day to shed the old – whatever 'the old' means for you."

Sarah Ban Breathnach

Date: _____

Moment of Awesome

"Courage is the power to let go of the familiar."

Raymond Lindquist

Date: _____

Moment of Awesome

"When I let go of what I am, I become what I might be. When I let go of what I have, I receive what I need."

Tao Te Ching

Date: _____

Moment of Awesome

"Open your arms to change, but don't let go of your values."

The Dalai Lama

Date:  _____

Moment of Awesome

"Study the past if you would define the future."

Confucius

Date: _____

Moment of Awesome

"Life moves forward. The old leaves wither, die and fall away, and the new growth extends forward into the light."

Bryant McGill

Date: _____

Moment of Awesome

"Making a big life change can be scary but living with regret is always scarier."

Unknown

Date: _____

Moment of Awesome

"Don't dwell on what went wrong. Instead, focus on what to do next. Spend your energy moving forward together towards an answer."

Denis Waitley

Date: _____

Moment of Awesome

"To help yourself, you must be yourself. Be the best that you can be. When you make a mistake, learn from it, pick yourself up, and move on."

Dave Pelzer

Date: _____

Moment of Awesome

"In three words I can sum up everything I've learned about life: it goes on."

Robert Frost

Date: _____

Moment of Awesome

"I demolish my bridges behind me…then there is no choice but to move forward."

Fridtjof Nansen

Date: _____

Moment of Awesome

"Life is like riding a bicycle, to keep your balance, you must keep moving."

Albert Einstein

Date: _____

Moment of Awesome

"Look forward, not behind. Your best days are still out in front of you. Be focused and keep your dreams ALIVE"

Adedayo Olabamiji

Date: _____

Moment of Awesome

"Do something today that your future self will thank you for."

Unknown

Date: _____

Moment of Awesome

"If you're not moving forward, you're falling back."

Sam Waterson

Date: _____

Moment of Awesome

"Every minute you spend in planning saves 10 minutes in execution; this gives you a 1000 percent return on energy."

Brian Tracy

Date: _____

Moment of Awesome

"Good fortune is what happens when opportunity meets with planning."

Thomas Edison

Date: _____

Moment of Awesome

"When we are no longer able to change a situation, we are challenged to change ourselves."

Viktor Frankl

Date: _____

Moment of Awesome

A year from now you will wish you had started today.

Karen Lamb

Date: _____

Moment of Awesome

"It doesn't matter where you are, you are nowhere compared to where you can go."

Bob Proctor

Date: _____

Moment of Awesome

"Man cannot discover new oceans unless he has the courage to lose sight of the shore."

Andre Gide

Date: _____

Moment of Awesome

"I can accept failure, everyone fails at something. But I can't accept not trying."

Michael Jordan

Date: _____

Moment of Awesome

"You miss 100 percent of the shots you never take."

Wayne Gretzky

Date: _____

Moment of Awesome

"The greatest mistake you can make in life is to be continually fearing you will make one."

Elbert Hubbard

Date: _____

Moment of Awesome

"Never too old, never too bad, never too late, never too sick to start from scratch once again."

Bikram Choudhury

Date: _____

Moment of Awesome

"If you run you stand a chance of losing, but if you don't run you've already lost."

Barack Obama

Date: _____

Moment of Awesome

"To create more positive results in your life, replace 'if only' with 'next time'."

Unknown

Date: _____

Moment of Awesome

"Use what talents you possess, the woods will be very silent if no birds sang there except those that sang best."

Henry van Dyke

Date: _____

Moment of Awesome

"By changing nothing, nothing changes."

Tony Robbins

Date: _____

Moment of Awesome

"One day your life will flash before your eyes. Make sure it's worth watching."

Unknown

Date: _____

Moment of Awesome

"Courage doesn't always roar. Sometimes courage is the little voice at the end of the day that says I'll try again tomorrow."

Mary Anne Radmacher

Date: _____

Moment of Awesome

"When in doubt, choose change."

Lily Leung

Date: _____

Moment of Awesome

"All great changes are preceded by chaos."

Deepak Chopra

Date: _____

Moment of Awesome

"Getting over a painful experience is much like crossing monkey bars. You have to let go at some point in order to move forward."

C.S. Lewis

Date: _____

Moment of Awesome

"You're braver than you believe, and stronger than you seem, and smarter than you think."

A. A. Milne

Date: _____

Moment of Awesome

"To improve is to change; to be perfect is to change often."

Winston Churchill

Date: _____

Moment of Awesome

"Taking a new step, uttering a new word, is what people fear most."

Fyodor Dostoyevsky

Date: _____

Moment of Awesome

"I'm looking forward to the future, and feeling grateful for the past."

Mike Rowe

Date: _____

Moment of Awesome

"Set your goal and keep moving forward."

Georges St-Pierre

Date:  _____

Moment of Awesome

"If you can't fly then run, if you can't run then walk, if you can't walk then crawl, but whatever you do you have to keep moving forward."

Martin Luther King Jr.

Date: _____

Moment of Awesome

"You are always a student, never a master. You have to keep moving forward."

Conrad Hall

Date: _____

Moment of Awesome

"Those who move forward with a happy spirit will find that things always work out."

Gordon B. Hinkley

Date: _____

Moment of Awesome

"If we fail to adapt, we fail to move forward."

John Wooden

Date: _____

Moment of Awesome

"Move forward with purpose."

Sherrilyn Kenyon

Date: _____

Moment of Awesome

"Go back?" he thought. "No good at all! Go sideways? Impossible! Go forward? Only thing to do! On we go!" So up he got, and trotted along with his little sword held in front of him and one hand feeling the wall, and his heart all of a patter and a pitter."

J. R. R. Tolkein

Date: _____

Moment of Awesome

"A clear vision, backed by definite plans, gives you a tremendous feeling of confidence and personal power."

Brian Tracy

Date: _____

Moment of Awesome

"Everything You've Ever Wanted Is On The Other Side Of Fear."

George Addair

Date: _____

Moment of Awesome

"I am thankful for all of those who said 'No' to me. It's because of them I'm doing it myself."

Albert Einstein

Date: _____

Moment of Awesome

"Successful men and women keep moving. They make mistakes but they don't quit."

Conrad Hilton

Date: _____

Moment of Awesome

"Success will never be a big step in the future. Success is a small step taken just now."

Unknown

Date: _____

Moment of Awesome

"You have to risk going too far to discover just how far you can really go."

T.S. Elliot

Date: _____

Moment of Awesome

"The first step toward success is taken when you refuse to be a captive of the environment in which you first find yourself."

Mark Caine

Date: _____

Moment of Awesome

"Challenges are what make life interesting and overcoming them is what makes life meaningful."

Joshua J. Marine

More Entrepreneur Tools, Guides, and Courses:

www.meganbrame.com
www.stopsuckingatbusiness.com
www.betterbizschool.com

Copyright © 2019 Megan Brame-Finkelstein/Meve LLC.

All rights reserved. No part of this book may be reproduced in any form on by an electronic or mechanical means, including information storage and retrieval systems, without permission in writing from the publisher, except by a reviewer who may quote brief passages in a review.

Cover images courtesy of Getty Images

www.ingramcontent.com/pod-product-compliance
Lightning Source LLC
Chambersburg PA
CBHW031443210526
45464CB00005B/2317